200
ACTIVITIES FOR PEOPLE WITH
ALZHEIMER'S/DEMENTIA

200
ACTIVITIES FOR PEOPLE WITH
ALZHEIMER'S/DEMENTIA

Experience Joy, Happiness,
Accomplishment, and Purpose through Activities

IN HIS NAME

BOOKLOGIX®
Alpharetta, GA

The resources contained within this book are provided for informational purposes only and should not be used to replace the specialized training and professional judgment of a healthcare professional. The author and publisher of this work cannot be held responsible for the use of the information provided. Always consult a licensed health professional before making any decision regarding treatment of yourself or others.

ISBN: 978-1-6653-0452-8

This ISBN is the property of BookLogix for the express purpose of sales and distribution of this title. The content of this book is the property of the copyright holder only. BookLogix does not hold any ownership of the content of this book and is not liable in any way for the materials contained within. The views and opinions expressed in this book are the property of the Author/Copyright holder, and do not necessarily reflect those of BookLogix.

♾This paper meets the requirements of ANSI/NISO Z39.48-1992 (Permanence of Paper)

030623

*Do not ask me to remember. Don't try to make me understand.
Let me rest and know you're with me. Kiss my cheek and hold my hand.*

*I'm confused beyond your concept. I am sad and sick and lost.
All I know is that I need you to be with me at all cost.*

*Do not lose your patience with me. Do not scold or curse or cry.
I can't help the way I'm acting, can't be different though I try.*

*Just remember that I need you, that the best of me is gone.
Please don't fail to stand beside me, love me 'til my life is gone.*

— Author unknown

CONTENTS

Creative Is as Creative Does

Playdough and Straws   2
Happy Faces   4
Things to Do with . . . Cereal Boxes (3 Activities)   5
Paint Chips (4 Activities)   6
Alcohol Ink Stamping (2 Activities)   8
Coloring/Painting (3 Activities)   10
Stenciling   12
Milk and Food Color Art   13
Painting with Feathers   14
Tape Art   16
Plastic Jug Ball Catcher   18
I'll Do One. . . Then You Do One!   19
Rubber Stamping   20
Decorating Clipboards   22
Message Rocks   23
Fabric Marker Art   24
Sand Art   25
Decorating Hats   26
Foam Stickers and More (3 Activities)   27
Tablet Art   29

Simple Activities

No Instructions Required (71 Activities)   32
Things to Do with Paper (21 Activities)   40
Items to Make with Paper Plates (8 Activities)   42
Enjoyable Bird Feeders (6 Activities)   43
Pipe Fitting   47
Prayer Box   48
Sock Warmers   49
Stamping with Pencil Erasers   50
Jeanne's Button Activity   51
Shaving Cream Art   52
Family Dry Erase Message Board   53

Around the House

Pets   56
Surprise Gifts   58
DVDs   59
Sensory Perception Bag   60
YouTube Is Your Friend   61

Sorting Laundry (3 Activities) 62

Pipe Cleaners! (4 Activities) 64

Seek and Find 66

Cup Decorating and Stacking 67

Sorting Coins 68

Fish Aquarium 70

Recycled Magazines (7 Activities) 71

String Scavenger Hunt 74

Memory Notebooks 75

Games and Puzzles

Jigsaw Puzzles 78

Make a Jigsaw Puzzle 79

Indoor Snowball Toss (5 Activities) 80

File Folder Games (6 Activities) 82

A Twist on "Simon Says" 86

Card Games (3 Activities) 87

Things to Do Outside

Nature Sightseeing 90

Walk on the Beach 92

Our Trips. . . Our Stories 94

Vehicles and More. 95

Seed Planting 96

Cell Phone Walk 97

Food for Foodies

Ziploc Bag Omelet(s) 100

Make and Decorate Cupcakes 102

Coffee Cup Microwave Scrambled Eggs 103

English Muffins Pizza 104

It's Not Just Pudding 105

Music to My Ears

Music! Music! Music! 108

Sing Along 109

Music Encouraging Movement 110

Musical Instruments: Shakers 111

HOPE IS NOT ABOUT
BELIEVING YOU CAN
CHANGE THINGS.

HOPE IS ABOUT
BELIEVING YOU CAN
MAKE A DIFFERENCE.

—VÁCLAV HAVEL

CREATIVE IS AS CREATIVE DOES

NO PRIOR ART EXPERIENCE NEEDED
"ART IS IN THE EYE OF THE BEHOLDER"
ART IS FOR ART'S SAKE AND IS TO BE ENJOYED

PLAYDOUGH AND STRAWS

A FUN, COLORFUL ACTIVITY

This activity will help with eye-hand coordination, fine motor skills and is a lot of fun!

SAFETY PRECAUTION!

✓ As the Loved One will be utilizing a variety of materials and small items, never leave the Loved One alone during this activity. It is a Loved One, caregiver participation activity.

SUPPLIES:

- Plastic table cloth to protect the work surface
- Colorful straws
- Uncooked pasta, Ziti or Rigatoni
- Playdough the size of 2 or 3 softballs
- Small colorful cake candles
- Decorated, colorful, pipe cleaners
- Blunt nosed scissors (child scissors)

DIRECTIONS:

- Place the table cloth on the flat work surface.
- Remove the Playdough from their containers.
- Squish the Playdough into one (1) or two (2) piles, the size of a softball.
- Slightly flatten the Playdough pile.
- Take out the straws the caregiver has already cut into various lengths.
- Place pipe cleaners into Playdough any which way.
- Place straw pieces over the pipe cleaners.
- Take Ziti or Rigatoni out of box.

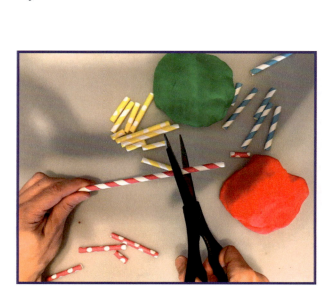

- Place anywhere in the Playdough.
- Press uncooked pasta (like a stamp) into the Playdough to make impressions and designs.
- Try all kinds of things, like looping pipe cleaners from one piece of pasta to another or printing out your name with straws.
- Take pictures of you, the Loved One and your Playdough project to show family and friends.

HAPPY FACES

There are many approaches to this project. You can simply make a smiling face on paper or use several different materials.

SUPPLIES:

- Magic Markers
- Crayons
- Stickers
- Acrylic Paint
- Any round object to trace
- Paper
- Card Stock
- Yellow Paper Plates
- Paint Brush
- Yellow Highlighter
- Pencil

DIRECTIONS:

- Look for examples of happy faces. Happy faces are everywhere!!!
- Look in magazines, newspapers and other printed materials.
- Look for stickers.
- Search online using the computer and copy them for your personal use.
- Option
  - Make a face on a yellow paper plate with a magic marker or acrylic paint.
- Option
  - Trace a round object on card stock or white paper with a marker. Pencil in a face. Use a yellow highlighter to color the entire face. Then go over the pencil marks using a dark marker.

THINGS TO DO WITH . . . CEREAL BOXES

Don't throw out your cereal boxes until you have tried some of these activities! They are free, skill building, and fun to make and play!

SAFETY PRECAUTION!

✓ Supervise the Loved One when using blunt scissors.

SUPPLIES:

- Cereal Boxes
  - 2 or more of the same cereal box
  - assortment of different cereals
- Children's blunt scissors

DIRECTIONS:
ACTIVITY NO. 1 MATCH GAME

- Play a match game with the fronts of the cereal boxes.

DIRECTIONS:
ACTIVITY NO. 2 I SPY

- Play "I Spy" games for example:
  - Find the corn chex, find the corn kernals.

DIRECTIONS:
ACTIVITY NO. 3 PUZZLE

- Make puzzles
- Cut the front of the box into puzzle pieces, the number and size depends on the skill level of the Loved One.

PAINT CHIPS

Caregivers can pick up a large variety of paint chip samples, free at paint stores and paint departments in large box stores such as Walmart, Lowes, etc. There are many different ways that paint chips can be used. Some are noted in this "paint chip" activity.

SAFETY PRECAUTION!

✓ When using scissors (preferably blunt nosed), magic markers and glue always supervise the Loved One.

SUPPLIES:

- Pick out an assortment of paint chip samples. Once you choose a color pick two (2) of the same color and shade and then pick out two (2) of an entirely different color and so on. Do not pick out a similar color or shade of the same color.
- Stickers
- Various colored magic markers
- Glue stick
- White or colored paper/card stock
- Blunt nosed scissors

DIRECTIONS:
ACTIVITY NO. 1 BOOKMARKS

- Make bookmarks by cutting paint chips to size and decorating with stickers.

DIRECTIONS:
ACTIVITY NO. 2 MATCHING GAME

- Play a matching game to match paint chips of the same distinctive color.

DIRECTIONS:
ACTIVITY NO. 3 PUZZLE

- Use two or more paint chips, line them up, draw a picture or design across them. Separate the chips and have the Loved One line them up like a puzzle.

DIRECTIONS:
ACTIVITY NO. 4 DESIGNS

Cut the paint chips into different sizes and shapes. Glue them onto a piece of paper to make a design.

ALCOHOL INK STAMPING

DECORATING TILES

This easy art project produces great results at a low cost. No one can make a mistake. Only lots of fun!

SAFETY PRECAUTION!

✓ Keep and store Alcohol Ink safely from the Loved One. When using, supervise the Loved One at all times. Do not permit the Loved One to spray the hair spray or lacquer spray on the final art piece.

SUPPLIES:

(Available at craft store)
- Cost: $10-$15
- Variety of alcohol ink colors (3 are enough to start)
- Alcohol-blending solution or rubbing alcohol
- Ink stamper and pads made for alcohol-ink use
- Square white tiles (4 ¼ inch or 6 inch)
- Small felt pads with sticky backing to use as feet
- Clear lacquer spray (or hairspray)
- Plastic mat to protect work surface

DIRECTIONS:
ACTIVITY NO. 1 INK DROP

- Clean the top surface of a tile with alcohol and paper towel.
- Place a white ink pad on the ink stamper.
- Apply 12-18 drops of one color ink on the pad surface, leaving space between drops.
- Dab the stamped pad on the white tile, leaving spaces. Allow ink to dry 20-30 seconds.
- Replace the ink pad with a clean one, and apply another color.

DIRECTIONS:
ACTIVITY NO. 2 INK FLOW

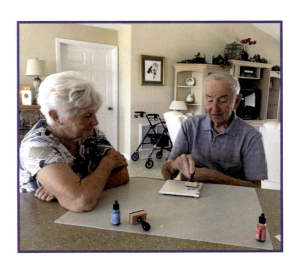

- Take a new tile and clean the surface, as before.
- Place a large drop (or several small drops) of ink directly on the tile.
- Then try one or more of these methods:
    - Tip the tile so the ink flows in different directions.
    - Blow the ink across the tile with a straw.
    - Spread the ink with a feather.
    - Use a toothpick or hard end of a paintbrush to run a line of ink across the tile.
- Let the ink dry before applying a different color.

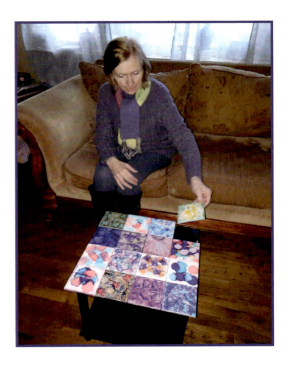

COLORING/PAINTING
"ARTISTIC TALENT NOT REQUIRED"

There are numerous activities and methods to color and paint. Included in this write up are only a few. All activities with thought and practice can be modified to the needs and capabilities of the Loved One.

SAFETY PRECAUTION!

✓ Take care that all coloring and painting products are non – toxic. Water based, washable paints are preferred. Keep open paint containers covered & secured when not in use. Supervise the Loved One at all times.

SUPPLIES:

- Include but not limited to:
    - Paper, tracing paper, cardboard & card stock
    - Water colors, finger paint & acrylic paint
    - Crayons, magic markers, colored pencils, colored bingo daubers
    - Paint brushes, Q-tips
    - Coloring books, clip art & computer applications
    - iPad, tablets

DIRECTIONS:
ACTIVITY NO. 1 COLORING

- Select topics that are enjoyable.
- Select pictures that are not too detailed.
- Select coloring books that are not childish.
- Try using clip art in the following manner:
    - Search for free clip art on the computer.
    - Select a picture and click on it.
    - Print out the picture.
    - If that does not work trace the picture.
- Some suggestions:
    - Coloring "inside the lines" is not essential.
    - Assist the Loved One slightly.
    - Reduce the number of choices confronting the Loved One by handing them one color at a time.
    - You do a small part then they do a part.
    - If that does not work see coloring modified Activity 2.

DIRECTIONS:
ACTIVITY NO. 2 MODIFIED COLORING WITH DAUBERS

- First make a simple line drawing.
- Utilize Bingo Daubers. Daubers are easier to hold.
- Select a Dauber and press it once on any line of the drawing.

DIRECTIONS:
ACTIVITY NO. 3 PAINTING

- Select painting projects that are enjoyable. Options include:
    - Paint kits. Kits are available in dollar type stores, big box stores such as Walmart, craft stores and online.
    - Paint books.
    - Make your own drawings to paint, utilizing free clip art (described in the coloring activity) on card stock.

STENCILING

This is an easy art form that gets very good results.

SUPPLIES:

- Stencils
- Stencil brush
- Bingo dauber
- Sponge roller
- Colored pencils, pens or felt marker
- Washable acrylic craft paints
- Stencil tape
- Card stock or paper
- Plastic protective covering for table if needed

DIRECTIONS:

- Select stencil.
- Tape it to paper or card stock.
- Select sponge roller or dauber.
- Apply paint to stencil.
- Or select pencil, pen or marker.
- Color in open area of stencil.
- You can just make art or create cards or signs.

MILK AND FOOD COLOR ART
EASY, FUN & EASY TO CLEAN UP

This activity is simple yet produces beautiful results. All items utilized most likely are found in your kitchen.

SUPPLIES:

- Milk
- Laundry Detergent
- Assorted Food Color
- Plastic Plate – Clear
- Small Plastic Bowl
- Q-tips

DIRECTIONS:

- Pour milk onto plastic plate.
- Place one or two drops of each food color on the milk.
- Pour a little detergent into a small bowl.
- Dip the Q-tip a little into the detergent.
- Touch the Q-tip with the detergent end on a color on the plate.
- Repeat for each color.
- Swirl the colors together.

PAINTING WITH FEATHERS

A NEW EXPERIENCE FOR MOST

You may be surprised at the many different ways each painting will vary whether one person does several different paintings or several different people each do one painting.

This type of painting does not require any art experience or ability. It is simply a fun easy project to do.

SUPPLIES:

- Plastic or paper table covering to protect the work surface
- Blank sheets of card stock or cardboard
- Washable, water soluble "finger" paint
- Package of feathers from craft store, Walmart, Target, etc.
- Paper plates
- Towel to clean up paint drops or spills
- Plastic spoon
- Paint stirrer

DIRECTIONS:

- The caregiver should prepare the paint by using the plastic spoon to scoop out each different color paint onto a paper plate.

- Select one feather and give it to the Loved One.
- Show or have the Loved One dip just the tip of the feather into one of the paint colors.
- If the paint appears to be too thick, thin it with water.
- Have the Loved One dab, swirl and drag the paint feather any which way across a blank piece of paper.
- A new feather should be used if the Loved One wants to change from one color to another.

TAPE ART

This is an activity that may end up looking a little like a stained glass window.

SAFETY PRECAUTION!

✓ Prepare the work area and the Loved One for working with paints and the likelihood of spills.

SUPPLIES:

- Canvas board – about 8''x10'' in size
- Scotch tape
- Acrylic jars of paint of different colors
- Paint brush
- Cup for water to clean brushes
- Plastic table cloth – something to protect the surface area
- Paper towels

DIRECTIONS:

- Place the canvas board on a table with protective covering.
- Pull off a length of tape and work with the Loved One to place it in any direction from one side to the other.

- Pull off another length of tape and tape it in a different direction on the canvas. Do not be worried if it intersects or overlaps other tape, this can be beneficial.
- Repeat the process while leaving a number of different areas of the canvas exposed.
- Put a little bit of one color of paint into the paint jar lid.
- Dip a paint brush into the paint and have the Loved One dab it on one or a few of the exposed canvas areas.
- Clean the brush with water and paper towel.
- Repeat the process in a different canvas area with a different color.
- Continue the process until all areas of the exposed canvas are covered.
- Let the paint dry completely.
- When dry, the Loved One can pull off each piece of tape and see the design

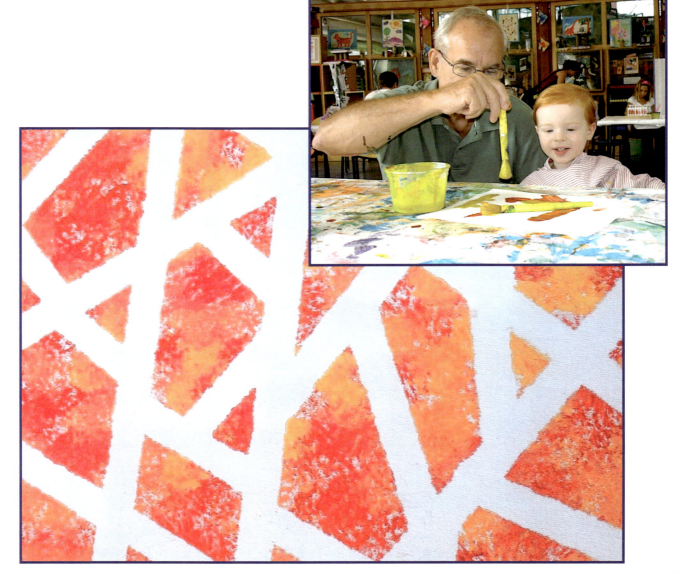

PLASTIC JUG BALL CATCHER

Many people enjoy playing catch. Traditionally we play catch with a glove and ball. In this activity the Loved One and caregiver will create a jug ball catcher and play catch with a very soft lightweight ball or round object.

SAFETY PRECAUTION!

✓ When you make your jug ball catcher, cover all rough or sharp edges with duct tape.
✓ When playing catch, only throw a very soft, lightweight object so that if it hits someone it will absolutely not hurt. Hard, rigid or weighted items should never be used.

SUPPLIES:

- Two (2) one (1) gallon plastic jugs
- Scissors
- Duct tape
- Very soft balls or make paper balls
- Stickers

DIRECTIONS:

- Before you start with this activity, cut off the bottom of the jug and tape the sharp edge with duct tape.
- The Loved One can now decorate the two (2) jugs with duct tape and stickers.
- Toss the soft object to each other and catch with the jug-catcher.

I'LL DO ONE. . . THEN YOU DO ONE!

A MAGNETIC POPSICLE STICK MATCHING GAME

This activity is easy, fun and as simple or difficult as you want for the Loved One. You will surely think of some different magnetic pieces to use to create a fun activity.

SAFETY PRECAUTION!

✓ Using small magnetic pieces can pose a choking hazard. Wooden pieces and popsicle sticks may look like food items. Do not leave the Loved One alone while making this activity.

SUPPLIES:

(Supplies can be found at Walmart/Dollar Tree)
- Large colored popsicle sticks/tongue depressors
- Magnetic strips with adhesive backing.
- Optional: other wooden shapes
- Cookie sheet
- Scissors

DIRECTIONS:

- Use an assortment of colored popsicle sticks.
- Stick magnetic pieces, strips or squares onto the backs of popsicle sticks.
- Stick them on a cookie sheet.
- Tell the Loved One that you will make a design and then below yours, he/she will copy it.

RUBBER STAMPING

Rubber stamping is a method to transfer images, words, or letters from a pre-made rubber stamp onto many different items. This activity can be modified in many ways to keep the Loved One involved and gain a sense of accomplishment. When selecting stamps consider ones with phrases that assist the Loved One to communicate. Example: "Thank You" or "I Love You".

SAFETY PRECAUTION!

✓ If you utilize a pre-prepared solution to clean the rubber stamp or the work area, read and follow the precautions on the container. Utilize acid free, non-toxic dye ink pads only.

SUPPLIES:

- Rubber stamp mounted on a block of wood
- Dye ink pad
- Copy paper, card stock and/ or greeting card
- Rubber gloves
- Mod Podge for finishing touches
- Plastic protector for the surface you will be working on

DIRECTIONS:

- Prepare a flat stable work area by covering it with a protector preferably plastic or a discardable table cloth.

- Take a piece of paper, card stock or greeting card and lay it out on the flat surface.
- Have the Loved One select a rubber stamp.
- Stamp the rubber stamp on to the dye-ink pad until the stamp is fully covered.
- The Loved One can stamp the inked rubber stamp where desired as often as desired.
- The Loved One can make cards, signs, messages or simply stamp, stamp, stamp. In later stages assistance can be provided at each step, even where to stamp, but if possible let them stamp, stamp, stamp.

DECORATING CLIPBOARDS

Clipboards are one of the most useful items you can imagine and such fun to personalize and make together. Using a clipboard to secure paper of any kind to the board, enables the Loved One to better manage tasks.

SAFETY PRECAUTION!

✓ Care should be taken relating to supplies that might go into the Loved One's mouth such as: paint, brushes, magic markers, glue stick, Mod Podge. Please do not leave the Loved One alone with these supplies.

SUPPLIES:

- Plain clipboards
- Covering to decorate the clipboard
- contact paper
- duct tape
- paints and brushes
- magic markers
- Download and print text, favorite verses, sayings and messages
- Glue stick
- Mod Podge for finishing touches
- Stencils
- Stamping supplies

DIRECTIONS:

- Decorate your clipboard with the supplies suggested.
- Print the Loved One's name on the board.
- After decorating use Mod Podge to protect your decorations.

MESSAGE ROCKS

Go on a hunt for flat rocks, clean them, paint them and give them as gifts. What a fun activity to do together with the Loved One.

SAFETY PRECAUTION!

✓ Be aware of the Loved One wandering as you go on your hunt!

SUPPLIES:

- Flat and smooth rocks
- Water, dish scrubber, towel
- Permanent markers or acrylic paints and brushes
- Mod Podge and brush to seal painting (Walmart, Target, Michaels, etc.)

DIRECTIONS:

- Wash and dry rocks completely.
- Paint anything on the rocks with markers or acrylic paint.
- Add single words or text with the permanent markers.
- When paint and markers are dry, apply 1-2 coats of Mod Podge to seal your work.

FABRIC MARKER ART

Drawing, coloring, stenciling and tracing on fabric can be fun, easy, inexpensive and rewarding.

SUPPLIES:

- Various colored fabric markers purchased at a craft store or craft department in a box store such as Walmart
- Fabrics such as:
    - T shirts
    - Hats
    - Sneakers
    - Pieces of fabric (light colored)
- Stencil(s) or item(s) to trace
- Pencil
- Scotch Tape

DIRECTIONS:

- Draw designs on a fabric, with the pencil, for the Loved One to color.
- Cut out an item to trace or use a stencil to outline a design on the fabric.
- If helpful consider taping the stencil or cut out on the fabric to hold it in place while sketching the design.
- Have the Loved One apply the color to the fabric.
- After done coloring, wait at least 24 hours, machine wash the fabric on gentle cycle and tumble dry on low.

SAND ART

SAFETY PRECAUTION!

✓ Take care with the use of glass containers, small objects and sand. All are potential hazards to the Loved One.

SUPPLIES:

- Clear plastic or glass bottle or jar with a secure top
- Colored sand
- Paper homemade funnel
- Spoon
- If desired other objects such as stones, shells, etc.
- Tape or glue gun

DIRECTIONS:

- Place funnel into the container.
- Spoon in colored sand, one color at a time.
- If desired as you spoon in the sand tilt the container to get a swirl design.
- Change colors and repeat the process until the container is full.
- Seal the top with a cap secured with tape or glue.

DECORATING HATS

JUST FOR FUN

There are many ways to do this activity and many reasons to decorate and use a "new" hat: a party for two, a birthday party, anniversary or other celebratory event. Some Loved Ones in their late stage of the illness may not be able to participate in the process of making the hat but thoroughly enjoy the activity and have a lot of fun wearing their hat!

SUPPLIES:

- Low cost hats are easy to find and use for this activity (Dollar Stores, Walmart, etc.)
- Card stock
- Playing cards
- Stickers
- Ribbon
- Magic markers
- Blunt nose scissors
- Scotch tape
- Various colors and designed duct tape
- Stapler
- Feathers

DIRECTIONS:

- Take the card stock and cut it into different sizes and shapes to be attached to the hat later.
- Decorate the card stock with magic markers and stickers.
- In various ways, staple the decorated card stock and playing cards to the hat.
- Consider additionally stapling feathers to the hat.
- Add ribbons and stickers.

FOAM STICKERS AND MORE

Make cards, signs, simple posters or decorate with stickers.

SUPPLIES:

- Foam sticker sheets
- Foam (or regular) stickers of all designs and types
- Stickers with numbers and letters
- Foam stickers craft kits
- Greeting cards with blank space inside
  - Birthday
  - Thank you
  - Anniversary
  - Holiday
- Colored card stock
- Plain or colored copy paper

DIRECTIONS: ACTIVITY NO. 1 GREETING CARDS

- Make a personalized greeting card.
  - Select a card with a lot of blank space for stickers.
  - Talk with the Loved One about who will get the card, what to say, and where to place the stickers.
  - The caregiver can peel off the sticker backing and hand it to the Loved One for placement wherever they want.
  - If the dexterity of the Loved One is not sufficient to handle a sticker, the caregiver can place the sticker and ask The Loved One to tap, tap, tap it into place.

DIRECTIONS: ACTIVITY NO. 2 DIRECTION SIGNS

- Make direction signs.
  - (One of the memories that stays a long time with the Loved One may be the ability to read. The Loved One can make direction signs that will assist them in the home. Examples include: Bathroom, Bedroom, Stop, Do Not Enter, etc.)
  - As a reference for the Loved One draft out, on a sheet of paper, what the signs will say.
  - Select the largest block letters you can find.
  - Lay out the letters for the Loved One to pick.
  - Peel and have the Loved One place and/or tap in place.

DIRECTIONS: ACTIVITY NO. 3 DECORATING WITH STICKERS

- Just for fun, stick stickers on a piece of paper, family picture frame, photo album, flower pot or other items. You can follow a theme for a holiday, a topic of interest to the Loved One such as sports, birds or flowers, or just to decorate.
  - You also can place stickers on things like glass doors to make them more visible.

TABLET ART

This shared activity is not only enjoyable for the Loved One, but the caregiver will also enjoy the process. It is simple, beautiful and enjoyable.

SUPPLIES:

- A tablet (iPad)
- A computer application on art
- Internet service

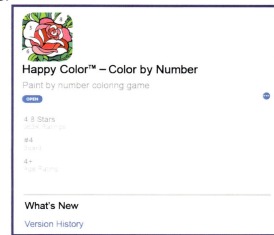

Happy Color™ – Color by Number
Paint by number coloring game

OPEN

4.8 Stars
563K Ratings

#4
Board

4+
Age Rating

What's New

Version History

DIRECTIONS:

- Open up your tablet.
- Go to a search engine such a Google.
- Type in free adult computer coloring books.
- Before sharing this activity the caregiver should try out a variety of applications and choose those that are the most workable for the Loved One.
- One feature that all applications possess is the ability to enlarge only a small part of the art piece to easily touch and color.
- Some suggested applications: Paint by Numbers Coloring Book, Bible Coloring & Coloring Games.

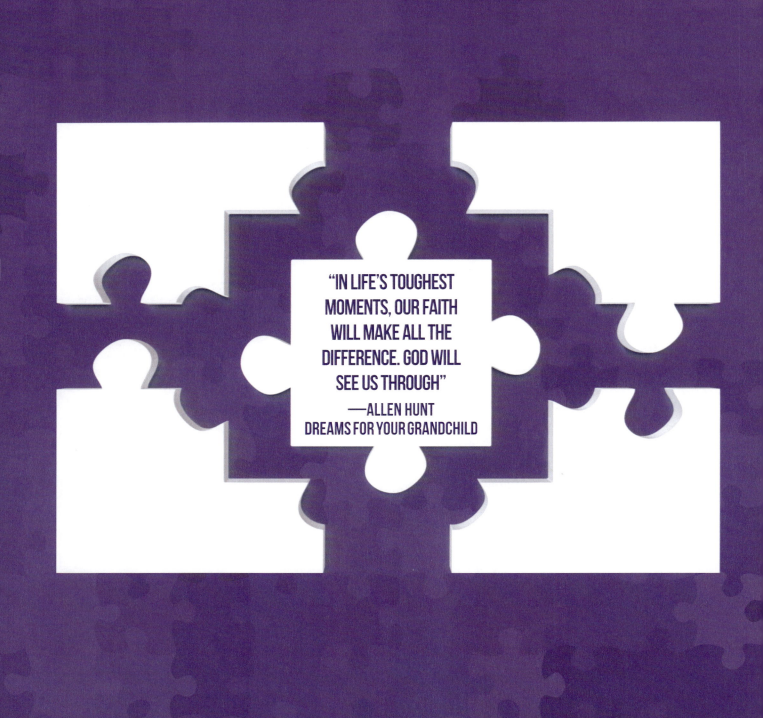

"IN LIFE'S TOUGHEST MOMENTS, OUR FAITH WILL MAKE ALL THE DIFFERENCE. GOD WILL SEE US THROUGH"

—ALLEN HUNT
DREAMS FOR YOUR GRANDCHILD

SIMPLE ACTIVITIES

LITTLE OR NO INSTRUCTION REQUIRED

NO INSTRUCTIONS REQUIRED

HUGGING

DANCING

HOLDING HANDS

DECORATING WITH DUCT TAPE

PLAYING WITH CARDS

BLOWING BUBBLES

ZOO VISIT

EGG DECORATING

PICKING PUMPKINS

HOUSEHOLD CHORES

CAKE IN A CUP

MAKE A SUNDAE

GOING TO THE PARK

TIME WITH GRANDCHILDREN

WALK THE DOG

BIRD HOUSE

BIRD FEEDER

LINCOLN LOGS

READING OUT LOUD

CUTTING & ARRANGING FLOWERS

MECHANICAL LIFE LIKE CAT

FINGER PAINTING

CHRISTMAS LIGHT TOUR

CELEBRATE HOLIDAYS

MAKE A GINGERBREAD HOUSE

PEANUT BUTTER & JELLY SANDWICH

QWIRKLE

FINGER PUPPETS

LOOK AT MAGAZINE(S)

PUTTING

WASHING DISHES

MATCHING SOCKS

POP 5/16" BUBBLE WRAP

CARING FOR PLANTS

SIMPLE CHAIR EXERCISE BIKE

CRAFT KITS

SWIFFERING

FAMILY GATHERINGS

WALKING IN THE RAIN

KINETIC SAND

PRAYING

FUN WITH HATS

WATCHING A PARADE

VIEWING A SUNSET

WATCHING GRASS GROW

DRESS UP FUNNY

PICK STRAWBERRIES

WATCH BOATS

COLORING

VISIT A FRIEND

PET A DOG

WEED

CHALK A FENCE OR WALK

GO FISHING

READ A SHORT BOOK TOGETHER

WATCH FIREWORKS

THROW A SNOWBALL

SHARE TIME CHILDREN

LOOK THROUGH OLD PHOTOS

GO TO CHURCH

HITTING BALLOONS

CELEBRATE A BIRTHDAY ANYTIME

WATCH PLANES LAND

BAKING BREAD

PLAYING WITH MODEL CARS

KNOCK KNOCK JOKES

BOWLING

WORM FARM

CLOUD WATCHING WITH IMAGINATION

WATCHING BASEBALL

SHUFFLE BOARD WITH A BROOM

THINGS TO DO WITH PAPER

TOSS CRUMPLED PAPER IN PAIL

TISSUE PAPER FLOWERS

BUTTERLY

POPSICLE STICK POPPERS

MAZE

FAN

DOODLE

PAPER HAT

TRACING

AIRPLANES

SCRAPBOOK

CHAINS

DOT TO DOT

STUFFED PAPER BAG

SUNCATCHER

BOOKMARKS

HOLE PUNCH DESIGN

SIMPLE LISTS

COFFEE FILTER PAINTING

CUP AND BALL GAME

TOILET PAPER ROLLER

ITEMS TO MAKE WITH PAPER PLATES

FLOWER

CATERPILLAR

FISH

HAPPY FACES

SNOWMAN

THANKFUL

TISSUE PAPER DESIGN

COLOR WHEEL

ENJOYABLE BIRD FEEDERS

There are a few different options when it comes to making bird feeders and a bird bath. If you do not want to make one, then buy one and place it where the Loved One can easily spend hours watching the birds. Just be patient as it may take several days for birds to find the new source of food and water.

SAFETY PRECAUTION!

✓ With some options you may be utilizing implements which pose a danger to the Loved One such as a hot glue gun. Never let the Loved One utilize these implements. Also, bird seed may look good to eat, but it is only for the birds. Supervise well.

ACTIVITY NO. 1 CUP AND SAUCER BIRD FEEDER AND BATH

Do you have old cups and saucers (or plates and small bowls) around the house? The birds will love the baths and feeders you can make from these items.

SUPPLIES:

- Cup, saucer, small bowl or dish from your cabinet or Dollar Tree
- Hot glue gun
- Outdoor table or stand
- Birdseed
- Water

DIRECTIONS:

- Choose a cup, saucer, small bowl or dish.
- Using a hot glue gun attach the cup to the saucer.
- Fill either the cup with bird seed and the saucer with water (or the opposite).
- Place on a table or stand outside so the Loved One can watch the birds "in action".

ACTIVITY NO. 2 PINE CONE BIRD FEEDERS

Simple and Quick To Make

SUPPLIES:

- Pine Cones
- Peanut butter
- Bird seed
- String or ribbon
- Blunt nose scissors
- Plastic spoon and knife
- Plastic table cover

DIRECTIONS:

- Cover the pine cone completely with peanut butter using the plastic knife and spoon.
- Make sure you press the peanut butter firmly into the cracks.
- Spread small piles of bird seed on the plastic table cover.
- Roll the pine cone in the bird seed to cover all around the cone.
- Attach a string and hang on a tree branch in sight of a window in your house.

ACTIVITY NO. 3 ORANGE CUP BIRD FEEDER

How simple can you get?

SAFETY PRECAUTION!

✓ The cutting of the orange should only be done by the caregiver.

SUPPLIES:

- An orange
- String
- Bird seed
- Plastic knife and spoon

DIRECTIONS:

- With the plastic knife the caregiver should cut the orange in half.
- Scoop the fruit out of the orange with the plastic knife and spoon.
- Attach string to the orange.
- Add bird seed.
- Hang the bird feeder outside.

ACTIVITY NO. 4 MILK CARTON BIRD FEEDER

SAFETY PRECAUTION!

- ✓ The cutting of the feeder openings should only be done by the caregiver.

SUPPLIES:

- Empty milk carton
- String
- Scissors
- Glass safe suction cup hook (option)

DIRECTIONS:

- The caregiver should cut out opening as shown.
- Attach string.
- Fill with seed and hang.

ACTIVITY NO. 5 BAGEL BIRD FEEDERS

SUPPLIES:

- Bagels
- Peanut butter
- Bird seed
- Plastic knife and spoon
- String

DIRECTIONS:

- Cut the bagels in half. This process is to be done only by the caregiver.
- Completely cover the flat side of the bagel with peanut butter.
- Dip or press the peanut butter side of the bagel on to a plate of bird seed.
- Tie the string through the hole in the bagel. Hang outside.

ACTIVITY NO. 6 CHEERIO BIRD FEEDER

SUPPLIES:

- Pipe cleaners
- Cheerios

DIRECTIONS:

- At one end of a pipe cleaner twist it into a loop so the Cheerios will not pass.
- Thread Cheerios onto the remainder of the pipe cleaner.
- Leave some of the pipe cleaner at the end.
- Attach it to the other end of the cleaner, another cleaner or just twist the top and make it in to a hanger.
- Shape or twist as desired.

PIPE FITTING

SAFETY PRECAUTION!

✓ Simply fit pieces of pipe together and take them apart.

SUPPLIES:

- 4 or more 6' sections of PVC pipe
- 10 or more PVC couplings
- 10 or more PVC elbows
- Pipe cutter
- Storage container

DIRECTIONS:

- Before working with the Loved One cut the 6' sections of PVC pipe into numerous smaller pieces.
- Place them into the storage container for easy access by the Loved One.
- The caregiver can start by connecting 2 pipe sections with a coupling
- The Loved One can continue with or without assistance to assemble all or many of the pipe sections.
- The caregiver can take cell phone pictures of the assembled sections.
- When the Loved One is no longer interested in assembling sections, it's time to have fun taking it all apart and putting the pieces back into the storage container.

PRAYER BOX

FUN TO MAKE AND A COMFORT TO HAVE

SUPPLIES:

- Altoids box
- White computer paper
- Glue stick
- Tacky glue
- Computer & printer
- Decorative buttons

DIRECTIONS:

- Empty the Altoids box.
- On the computer, type words in text boxes,
  for example:
  - Pray More Worry Less
  - When your head starts to worry and your
    mind can't rest, put your prayers down and let God do the rest.
- Print out words and cut out.
- Glue words on top of lid and underside of lid.
- Decorate with buttons, etc. as you like.
- Write prayers on small rectangles of paper that fit in the box.
- The Prayer Box is easy to carry with you wherever you go.
  Let the Loved One pick out a prayer and read it together.

SOCK WARMERS

Cold hands, frozen toes, a tummy ache, a warm snuggler … sock warmers are just for you and the Loved One to make and use! This is an easy gift idea as well!

SAFETY PRECAUTION!

✓ Be sure and stay with the Loved One while doing this activity. The rice is edible but raw rice may cause stomach aches if a quantity of rice is ingested. After making the sock warmer, test the time in the microwave so your sock isn't too hot to touch.

SUPPLIES:

- Socks – colorful tube or knee socks
   - Dollar Tree, Walmart or ones you already have
- Uncooked rice
- Funnel
   - Dollar Tree or homemade with card stock

DIRECTIONS:

- Using a funnel, fill a tube sock or knee sock with rice.
- Fill 2/3 full, leaving room to tie a tight knot at the opening of the sock.
- When ready to use, put in the microwave for 30 plus seconds to warm it up.
- Because of its long shape, it's perfect for laying across stomachs, on limbs and across the back of your neck.

STAMPING WITH PENCIL ERASERS

Make your own stamp pads using pencil erasers and create beautiful pictures together with the Loved One.

SAFETY PRECAUTION!

✓ Watch for paint and pencils going into mouths! Supervise! Use washable paint in case it gets on other items.

SUPPLIES:

- Inexpensive sponges
- Small plastic containers for each sponge
- Poster paint
- Cardstock or canvas board
- Optional: plain gift boxes, white wrapping paper
- Pencils with erasers on end
- Water and paper towels for cleanup
- Old newspapers for table protection

DIRECTIONS:

- Prepare your work space with newspapers.
- Lay out paper/item you will paint.
- Cut sponges to fit plastic containers.
    - One sponge per container.
- Dampen sponges with a little water.
- Dab paint onto sponge.
    - Use a different paint per sponge.
- Work paint into sponge.
- Using the eraser on the end of a pencil, dab the painted sponge and then dab the paper.
    - Use a different pencil for each color or wipe eraser clean after each paint.
- Make a design of choice.

JEANNE'S BUTTON ACTIVITY

Jeanne created this activity for her Loved One, Chuck, and it became one of his favorites.

SAFETY PRECAUTION!

✓ As most buttons are small this is a 1 to 1 person activity which requires the caregiver's participation and supervision.

SUPPLIES:

- Plenty of old buttons
- Container to store the buttons
- 6 small plastic bowls (all different colors if possible)
- Notecards or Post-it Notes to label the bowls accordingly.

DIRECTIONS:

- Jeanne often sorted the buttons with Chuck, in some of the following ways:
    - Dark colors
    - Light colors
    - Flat buttons
    - Raised buttons
    - 4 Hole buttons
    - 2 Hole buttons
- Label the bowls appropriately.
- Depending on the Loved One's skill level:
    - The caregiver can select a button and ask the Loved One in which bowl the button should be placed.
    - The Loved One can also select a button and make the decision on their own where the button belongs.

SHAVING CREAM ART

Easy to do, fun activity with little preparation time.

SAFETY PRECAUTION!

✓ This activity should be done in the kitchen area and near the sink. Make sure you have all your supplies at the table before you start. The caregiver will not want to leave the table before the completion of the activity.

SUPPLIES:

- Glass top table
- Plenty of terry cloth towels
- Some paper towels
- Men's shaving cream (Not menthol shaving cream)

DIRECTIONS:

- This activity should be done with the Loved One seated at the table.
- Take the shaving cream and spread it out on the glass top table to any size or shape you desire. The Loved One will enjoy this!
- Wipe off your hands with the towel as often as needed.
- With your fingers, draw, doodle, or scribble on the shaving cream "till your heart's content!"

FAMILY DRY ERASE MESSAGE BOARD

A Family Message Board is a great visual reminder of important things about each day! You and the Loved One can work on it together, talk about important days, family photos and personalize it as much as you want.

SAFETY PRECAUTION!

✓ Be sure to supervise the Loved One with the dry erase markers and the glue stick.

SUPPLIES:

- Large picture frame, preferably with Plexiglass (Dollar Tree)
- Dry erase markers
- Colored paper
- Calendar
- Stickers
- Glue stick
- Blunt nose scissors
- Magazines
- Photos

DIRECTIONS:

- Type or write the headings on the colored paper and decorate, or use letters cut out from a magazine.
- Glue headings on the back of the glass.
- Put frame back together.
- Using a dry erase marker, write on top of frame's glass each day.
- Heading suggestions:
    - Our Calendar
    - Our Plans for Today
    - Grocery List
    - Star of the Day (use a picture of a relative or friend)
    - Message of the day

I CAN DO EVERY-THING THROUGH CHRIST WHO GIVES ME STRENGTH

—PHIL. 4:13

AROUND THE HOUSE

MANY ACTIVITIES CAN BE STRUCTURED WITHIN THE HOUSE
AND WITH ITEMS FOUND AROUND THE HOUSE.

SOME ACTIVITIES ARE JUST FOR ENJOYMENT WHILE
OTHERS ARE ORIENTED TO PROVIDE LOVED ONES
A SENSE OF ACCOMPLISHMENT.

PETS

Any living animal as well as inanimate animals, such as stuffed or mechanical animals, can be a cherished pet and provide hours of enjoyment for the Loved One and caregiver. (Consideration should be given to the additional time and resources care of a pet may have on the already heavy demands of the caregiver.)

SAFETY PRECAUTION!

✓ Care must be taken – pets can be a tripping hazard or may frighten the Loved One.

SUPPLIES:

- Pets may include: dogs, cats, tropical fish, birds, rabbits, hamsters and more.
- Accessories to care for pets. Some pet accessories may be costly depending on the type of pet selected.

DIRECTIONS:

- Consideration should be given to the Loved One's ability to participate in the care and enjoyment of the pet.
- Alternatives to owning a pet should be considered. Alternative considerations include:
  - Taking trips to an animal shelter. Talk with them about what you are doing and ask if there is any volunteer work the Loved One can do. Shelters often care for many kinds of animals other than dogs and cats, that are small, docile and in need of attention.

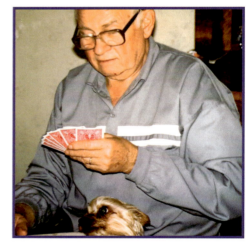

  - A neighbor might have a pet that is suitable and has the temperament that will bring joy to the Loved One for short periods of time. They may visit your home or you may visit theirs. Take care to ensure that the pet's behavior and characteristics will not scare or harm the Loved One.
  - Take trips to pet stores or zoos. While there, talk about the animals with the Loved One, and take

pictures with your phone. Show and talk about the pictures later. You can also make a memory book of your trip with printed photos.

- Many Loved Ones enjoy stuffed, life-like or mechanical animals. There are a number of them on the market developed for individuals with Alzheimer's. Many Loved Ones will treat the model animal as a live pet and caregivers often follow this behavior. It is ok. Enjoy the moment.

NOTE TO CAREGIVER:

• There are wonderful YouTube or Google animal clips you can watch. Just type in the kind of animal you or the Loved One enjoys.

YouTube suggestions include:
- "Kids and dogs bath time."
- "Sweet mama dog interacting with child."
- "Unbelievable unlikely animal friendships."
- "Funny guilty dog compilations."
- "Funny cat compilation."

SURPRISE GIFTS

FUN FOR EVERYONE

Most of us enjoy gifts, and surprise gifts are often the best! Loved Ones often enjoy surprise gifts more than most. This activity is one that the caregiver does for the Loved One and not with the Loved One.

SAFETY PRECAUTION!

✓ Many gifts work well as long as they are safe for the Loved One.

SUPPLIES:

- Gift bags
- Wrapping paper
- Bows
- Scotch tape
- Scissors
- Small gifts, such as crayons, photos, candy, cookies and holiday related items

DIRECTIONS:

- Select a gift.
- Wrap the gift simply or as ornately as you wish.
- Share the joy the Loved One gets as they open their gift.

DVDS
EASY TO USE AND HELPFUL

A great alternative to TV. When the caregiver utilizes DVDs they control what is being watched. The Loved Ones enjoy DVDs because they are not interrupted by commercials.

SAFETY PRECAUTION!

✓ Please avoid DVD topics that are too childish or contain violence of any type. Preview all DVDs!!

SUPPLIES:

- Computer or DVD player
- DVDs purchased in a store or online. Also check if your local library has a DVD loaner program.
- Some DVD recommended topics include:
  - Victor Borge
  - I Love Lucy
  - Gigglewiththegoats.com
  - Sports
  - Animals
  - Lunch Break with Tony (videorespite.com)

DIRECTIONS:

- Select a DVD and play

SENSORY PERCEPTION BAG

A SENSORY ACTIVITY TO DO USING THINGS FROM AROUND YOUR HOUSE

There are many items around the house that you can put into a decorative bag that the Loved One will enjoy holding one item at a time. Squeezing, stroking and manipulating are activities that could bring the Loved One moments of peace and calm.

SAFETY PRECAUTION!

✓ Be sure to supervise the Loved One when using small items.

SUPPLIES:

- Large gift bag
- Assortment of items from around your house
- Some suggested items:
  - Scarf, silk-like
  - Tie
  - Cotton balls in a Ziploc bag
  - Soft dog toy
  - Scrub sponge
  - Balled up tissue paper
  - Ribbon
  - Soft toys
  - Small plastic container and lid containing smaller objects like a: smooth stone, palm cross, and a large button

DIRECTIONS:

- Place all the items in the large decorative gift bag.
- Have the Loved One select one item from the bag.
- Encourage the Loved One to feel, manipulate, rub and move the item through their fingers.
- You may want to show or assist the Loved One in ways to perceive the feeling of the item.
- If the Loved One is disinterested in the item have him/her set it aside and select another item.
- Take your time. As long as the Loved One is interested in holding the item wait before selecting another item.
- Select another item.

YOUTUBE IS YOUR FRIEND
. . .AND SIMILAR TECHNOLOGY

When utilizing technologies like YouTube the caregiver is controlling the material to be reviewed by the Loved One.

SAFETY PRECAUTION!

✓ Preview all material to insure it is not frightening or contains violence.

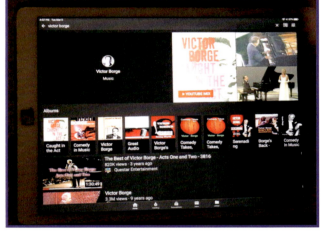

SUPPLIES:

• Computer or Tablet device
• Wi Fi

DIRECTIONS:

• Turn on the device.
• Click on YouTube icon or use a Google type search and type in YouTube.
• When YouTube site comes up click on the magnifying glass at the top right hand corner of the screen.
• Type in the item or topic of interest to be viewed.
• Some suggested topics include:

- Music comedy
- Marx Brothers
- Victor Borge
- Classical music in the key of comedy
- Unusual Music
- Water glasses secret performer
- Street perform Wintergatan – Marble Machine
- Piano street performers
- Pets
- Pet animals getting a bath.

- Fun dog tricks with Roque & Ruger
- Grandparents/Kids
- Brian Kinder, Grandma, Grandpa song
- Grandparents day song
- Little big shots by Steve Harvey
- Sports
- Golf top 10
- Bowling top 10
- Football top 10

• Other ideas to explore:

- Christmas
- Cars
- Dancing/songs

- Old tv comedies, shows, commercials

SORTING LAUNDRY

ENCOURAGES LOVED ONE TO BE HELPFUL

These are just a few ideas to get you started on a sorting activity. You can modify the activity to match the abilities and interest of the Loved One. You can also create other sorting activities such as flatware, napkins, plastic dishes, cards by color or numbers, etc. Also see activity titled Sorting Coins.

SAFETY PRECAUTION!

✓ If necessary to avoid any tripping or falling hazards, remove large bulky items from the laundry such as, sheets or bathrobes. Preferably have the Loved One sit while sorting.

SUPPLIES:

- Laundry
- Laundry basket
- Safe place for the Loved One to sort (Kitchen table, couch, etc.)

DIRECTIONS: ACTIVITY NO. 1 SORTING DIRTY CLOTHES

- Have the Loved One look at each piece of clothing and tell or show which pile is dark or light laundry.
- If possible have the Loved One put sorted colors into the washer.

DIRECTIONS: ACTIVITY NO. 2 SORTING HIS AND HERS

- The clean and dry laundry now can be sorted into "his & hers" piles.
- Hold up a piece of laundry and ask the Loved One if it should be in his or her pile.

DIRECTIONS: ACTIVITY NO. 3 MORE SORTING

- Go to the pile of the Loved One.
- Holding up one item of laundry at a time sort like items into like piles. Example – tee shirts into one pile, socks into another.
- The Loved One simply tells you by word or gesture which pile to place like items.
- If possible and safe the Loved One can assist the caregiver put their sorted, clean laundry "away".
- At the conclusion of the activity thank the Loved One for her/ his help. This gesture will help validate how important their assistance is to you and show appreciation for their help.

PIPE CLEANERS!

Have you ever thought of fun things to do with pipe cleaners? They are great for fine motor skills, feeling silly, and cheap to buy! Here are a few ideas for this together activity. https://www.pinterest.com/explore/pipe/cleaners/

SAFETY PRECAUTION!

✓ Watch out for the pipe cleaners going into mouths. The ends have a sharp wire but it can be bent a little or taped to eliminate the sharpness. With supervision, these are fun and easy activities for you and the Loved One.

SUPPLIES:

- Assortment of pipe cleaners
- Old spice jar or Pringles type can
- Colander
- Strong magnet (wand if possible)
- Clear plastic water or soda bottle
- Children's blunt scissors

DIRECTIONS: ACTIVITY NO. 1 PIPE CLEANER SORT

- Cut the pipe cleaners in half.
- Use an old spice jar, or Pringles type can.
- With permanent markers, color the holes to match the pipe cleaners.
- Stick the pipe cleaners in the holes.

DIRECTIONS: ACTIVITY NO. 2 PIPE CLEANER STICK-UM

- Use a kitchen colander and stick the pipe cleaners into holes.
- Create a design or just stick into holes.
- It's a win-win activity and great skill building.

DIRECTIONS: ACTIVITY NO. 3 PIPE CLEANER STICK PEOPLE/ANIMALS

- Bend and twist pipe cleaners to make people/animals/a design.
- To create wiggle worms, wrap pipe cleaners around a pencil.
- Talk about your silly creation.

DIRECTIONS: ACTIVITY NO. 4 MAGNETIC PIPE CLEANER FUN

- Cut pipe cleaners into different lengths, 1-2" long and put into an empty water or soda bottle. Secure the lid.
- Place a strong magnet or magnetic wand on the outside of the bottle and move it around to move the pipe cleaners.
- Choose a color to try to move each time.
- It's magic… have fun!

SEEK AND FIND

This activity is simple and rewarding for most Loved Ones. It does not require much preparation and can be done at a moment's notice. There are a variety of different ways to carry out this activity depending on the Loved One's interest and abilities.

SAFETY PRECAUTION!

✓ Be aware and take preventive care to insure that the activity does not result in the Loved One tripping or falling. Take precautions as necessary.

SUPPLIES:

• Cellphone or tablet with a camera

DIRECTIONS:

• Walk around the room with the Loved One. Sitting in a favorite room is also ok.

• Look around the room, point out a single item at a time and talk about it. Items such as a family photo, picture, plant or lamp.
• With your cellphone or tablet camera take a picture of the individual item. Clearly frame the item so the item is all that is in the picture.
• Once you have completed your photo tour, look at a single photo, show it to the Loved One and talk about it.
• Ask the Loved One to look around the room and find the item in the room that matches the photo.
• If the Loved One has difficulty finding the items give hints.
• In some situations it may be necessary to bring the Loved One to the item, place the photo near it and ask: Is this a match- do they look alike?
• Whatever the Loved One answers can always be responded to in a positive manner by simply saying "I can see how you answered that way".

CUP DECORATING AND STACKING

This activity is easy to do, inexpensive, very popular and enjoyable. Many of us over a long time have enjoyed games where we see how high we can stack something and there has always been someone around that cannot wait to knock the stack down.

SAFETY PRECAUTION!

✓ Only do this activity while the Loved One is sitting down.

SUPPLIES:

- Any size paper or plastic cup that you can color on with a sharpie, 3 oz. bathroom cups are popular. They can be stacked high and wide in a small space.
- Sharpie or permanent marker
- A flat surface to work on
- Possibly a small very soft toy that if thrown will not hurt anyone or anything.

DIRECTIONS:

- Separate the cups and draw a decoration on each cup with a colored permanent marker. Do not be overly concerned with how the Loved One decorates them.
- Decorate as many as you want, 30 cups per person will not be too many.
- Line up 6-8 cups in front of the Loved One on a stable flat surface.
- Let the Loved One start stacking upon the base of 6-8 cups. You may have to start the stacking so the Loved One will see how to stack the cups.

SORTING COINS

This is a fun and productive activity for the Loved One to do. Please remember to disinfect and dry the coins prior to the Loved One handling them.

SAFETY PRECAUTION!

✓ Coins may be a potential choking hazard and may carry harmful germs. Clean the coins thoroughly and always supervise the Loved One during this activity. Following the activity, put all the coins away for safe keeping. Do not heat water on stove, use warm water from the faucet.

SUPPLIES:

- An assortment of coins
- Clean plastic unbreakable bowls. Four (4) medium size bowls of different colors and one (1) large bowl
- One (1) medium size cooking pot or pan
- A pair of rubber gloves
- Disinfectant, such as Lysol
- Paper or cloth towel
- Hand sanitizer

DIRECTIONS:

- Using the pair of rubber gloves, clean and dry the assortment of coins. One way to do so is as follows:
  - Place the assortment of coins in to the cooking pot.
  - Liberally add the disinfectant.
  - Add warm water to the pot above the level of the coins.
  - Mix the coins around in the pot.
  - Let the coins sit in the cleaner for a few minutes.
  - Pour out the disinfectant & water solution and rinse the coins two (2) or three (3) times.
  - Dry with a towel.

- Place the clean, dry assortment of coins in the large plastic bowl.
- Set out four (4) different colored medium size bowls.
- Show and direct the Loved One how to put like denominations in each bowl.
- If the Loved One is confused by seeing a large assortment of coins, set the large bowl aside and hand a coin, one (1) at a time to the Loved One, to deposit it in a bowl with the same denomination.
- If necessary you can prompt the Loved One by saying, "put the coin in the red bowl, or blue bowl as the case may be.
- Another prompt could be to write out the color on a card stock and place or tape it to a bowl. Asked that the coin be placed "in the red bowl". (Many Loved Ones retain the ability to read long after they forget "their colors".)

FISH AQUARIUM
SETTING UP AND MAINTAINING

If the caregiver has no prior experience it is recommended that a purchase of a 3 to 5 gallon aquarium is the way to start.

SUPPLIES:

- Aquarium kit which should include:
  - The tank with a cover
  - A filter system with cartridge
  - Light
  - Instructions
- Gravel designated for aquarium use
- Plastic plants
- Air pump if not in kit
- Water conditioner for aquariums
- Heater
- Thermometer
- Fish food

DIRECTIONS:

- Select a location for your tank where it is easily visible by the Loved One.
- Wash the inside of the aquarium and all items that will be inside it with warm water.
- Wash and rinse the gravel several times.
- Fill the tank about halfway with room temperature tap water.
- Set up your filter, heater and air pump in the tank.
- Fill the remainder of the tank with water.
- Add water conditioner according to the instructions.
- Wait 48 hours to give the aquarium time to clear and stabilize. It is normal for the water to be cloudy for a day or so.
- Now you can go to the pet store and purchase fish.
- Talk to someone who knows all about the different kinds of fish.
- Start with only a few fish. You can always add more later.
- Feed the fish as instructed.
- Enjoy.

RECYCLED MAGAZINES

Magazines around your house? Here are activities to do with old magazines! Fun, easy, almost free, no right or wrong, and using lots of different skills. We've included many different activities, but it is also fun for mid to late stage Loved Ones to flip through magazines. You will notice a smile when they see something familiar.

SAFETY PRECAUTION!

✓ It is recommended to use children's blunt scissors and glue sticks rather than liquid glue, but either may look like food, so do not leave the Loved One alone with these items.

SUPPLIES:

(Used for all the suggested activities)
- Magazines
  - Family Circle and Women's Day are good for pets, simple foods and large letters
  - Better Homes & Garden is good for garden and home pictures
  - Specialized magazines for golf, fishing, cars, sports, etc. have great pictures
- Children's blunt scissors (fingers for tearing when scissors can't be used)
- Glue sticks
- Paper… construction, card stock, computer paper
- Ziploc type plastic baggies

Draw a Face

DIRECTIONS: ACTIVITY NO. 1 MAGAZINE ART

- Decide if you want to make crazy people or crazy animals. Example: Draw the shape of a man's head.
- In a magazine, find and cut out different eyes, ears, body, legs, etc.
- Glue onto the man's head, making a very crazy person.

DIRECTIONS: ACTIVITY NO. 2 WORD HUNTS

- Word hunts and making silly sentences are fun ways to keep vocabulary and reading skills alive.
- Cut medium to large size words out of your magazine.
- Put them together to make silly sentences.
- Glue onto paper.
- Read and talk about them together.

DIRECTIONS: ACTIVITY NO. 3 COLLAGES

- Decide on the theme of your collage.
- Cut out pictures in your magazines that fit your theme.
- Glue pictures onto a piece of poster board or card stock.
- Label the pictures for the Loved One.

DIRECTIONS: ACTIVITY NO. 4 STORIES

- Look through magazines and find pictures you will like to use.
- The collection of pictures can be all one theme, very random, or just ones the Loved One wants to cut out.
- After you have the pictures, put them together to tell a story.
- You can also tell a story about just one of the pictures.
- The pictures can remain the same but the stories can vary each time.

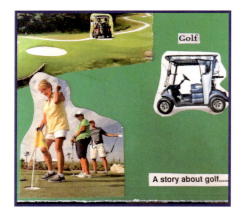

DIRECTIONS: ACTIVITY NO. 5 "WHAT IS IT?"

Just for fun guessing game!
- Cut out a picture of one item, such as a dog.
- Cover part of the picture with a blank paper.
- Ask the Loved One to guess what the picture is.
- Show more of the picture until the Loved One can guess what it is.

DIRECTIONS: ACTIVITY NO. 6 PUZZLES

From very simple to difficult, you can make puzzles for the Loved One.

- Cut out pictures, depending on the stage of the Loved One, a simple single object picture for a later stage Loved One, and with more details for earlier stage.
- Glue picture onto cardboard or card stock.
- After pictures dry, cut into pieces. The number of pieces depends on the stage of the Loved One.
- Each puzzle can be put into a Ziploc bag for storage.

DIRECTIONS: ACTIVITY NO. 7 MATCHING GAME

Hooray for duplicate advertisements! This activity can be adapted for each individual with lots of success.

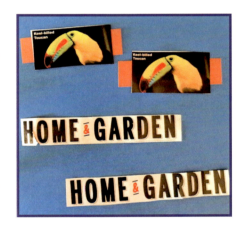

- In your magazines, look for duplicate (2) matching products.
- Repeat this with several different products.
- Place them all together in a pile.
- Pick out one item and ask the Loved One to find the match.

STRING SCAVENGER HUNT

A new version of a scavenger hunt just for the Loved One. He/she will follow the string and find a prize. Sounds fun!!!

SAFETY PRECAUTION!

✓ Be aware of the physical limitations of the Loved One when deciding where to put your string/ribbon. Such as: can they keep their balance and bend down to look under tables or chairs, and is the area free and clear of obstacles that might cause falls?

SUPPLIES:

- String or ribbons
    - enough string to wrap around a few chairs, tables, door knobs
- Small prize in a bag or box at the end of the hunt

DIRECTIONS:

- Decide how challenging you can make the course depending on the skill level of the Loved One.
- Decide on the prize for the treasure at the end of the hunt such as:
    - a treat to eat or maybe a small gift.
- To begin, tie your string/ribbon around something, such as a door knob or chair. Mark it with something such as a bow, balloon or sign.
- Continue stringing your string/ribbon around furniture in your house.
- Decide where the string ends and the prize will be hidden.
- Tell the Loved One to hold onto the string and follow it until they find the prize.

MEMORY NOTEBOOKS

KEEPING MEMORIES ALIVE

Memory books are not only enjoyable to make, but the Loved One will often carry a book or two with them and flip through the pages repeatedly. Each book should focus on one subject or theme such as cars, pets, family, dolls, old toys. The theme should be one the Loved One most enjoyed in the past.

SUPPLIES:

- Small journal notebook. (Dollar type stores are a good source)
- Magazine pictures (Group them into categories or subjects)
- Photos
- Calendar pictures
- Blunt nose scissors, glue, tape, stapler, magic marker or pen

DIRECTIONS:

- Choose a single theme.
- From your collection of supplies layout a number of pictures in one category.
- Pick out one photo or picture at a time and show it to the Loved One.
- If the Loved One shows an interest in the picture put it aside to be used.
- Take the pictures or photos the Loved One enjoyed the most and glue, tape or staple them into the notebook.
- Often you can put one larger picture or photo on each page which is easier for the Loved One to focus.
- With a magic marker, in bold print, identify the picture.
- With family pictures print their name.

"WE MUST
ACCEPT FINITE
DISAPPOINTMENT
BUT NEVER
LOSE INFINITE HOPE"
—DR. MARTIN LUTHER KING JR.

GAMES AND PUZZLES

JUST FOR FUN

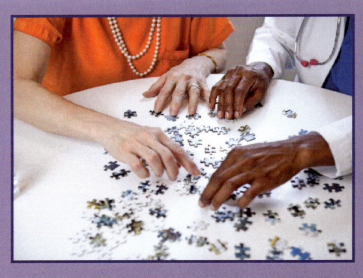

JIGSAW PUZZLES

FUN FOR EVERYONE

SUPPLIES:

- Store bought jigsaw puzzles
- Solid flat surface
- Comfortable chairs for the caregiver and the Loved One to sit next to each other

DIRECTIONS:

- Puzzles should be appropriate to the abilities of the Loved One and not childish.
- Start with the easiest puzzle you can obtain. Example: a 24 piece puzzle.
- Show the Loved One the completed puzzle.
- Have a picture of the completed puzzle as a guide for the Loved One.
- Take the puzzle apart.
- If the puzzle is too easy, then try a slightly more difficult puzzle. Example: a 36 piece puzzle.
- If the puzzle is too difficult try leaving a few pieces already together before giving it to the Loved One.

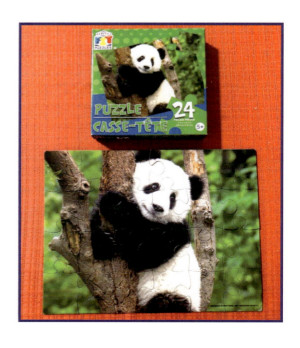

MAKE A JIGSAW PUZZLE

Specialty puzzles with only a few pieces can be very expensive to purchase. Making your own is inexpensive, relevant and simple. This project is just for the caregiver or someone other than the Loved One to make for the continued use and enjoyment of the Loved One.

SUPPLIES:

- Peel and stick foam sheets
- Personal photos, cards or pictures
- Jigsaw template for a 6 to 9 piece puzzle (you can go online for samples of templates)
- Scissors
- Scotch tape

DIRECTIONS:

- Draw your own jigsaw template to the size of the foam sheet you will be using.
- Peel the coating off the sticky side of the foam sheet.
- Select a photo or picture.
- Apply the picture to the sticky side of the foam sheet.
- Turn the foam sheet over.
- Tape the template to this side.
- With scissors cut along the template line

INDOOR SNOWBALL TOSS

FUN ANY TIME OF THE YEAR

This activity works well for an individual or for groups of any size.

SAFETY PRECAUTION!

✓ Please make sure your artificial snowballs are light and soft so as not to injure anyone or break anything.

SUPPLIES:

- Decorated (or plain) box or trash can
- Artificial snowballs (available online; brands include Selftek 50 fake snowballs, for $20)
- Or… for homemade snowballs:
  - White tube socks
  - Sheets of paper (cotton balls or fiberfill work too)

DIRECTIONS: HOMEMADE SNOWBALLS

- Stuff crumpled paper (or other material) into the toe end of a sock.
- Shape into the form of a snowball.
- Cut off the sock between the toe and the heel, leaving enough material to either tie or sew the end together.
- Trim excess material.

ACTIVITY NO. 1

- Give each Loved One several snowballs.
- One at a time (or however it works out), have players toss their snowballs into a decorated box or trash can.
- Score 1 point for hitting the box.
- Score 2 points for getting a snowball into the container.
- For group play, players might "compete", or they can "always tie", so everyone is a winner!

ACTIVITY NO. 2

- Stack small plastic or paper cups into a pyramid. (See cup stacking activity)
- Have Loved Ones throw snowballs at the stack and try to knock down the cups.

ACTIVITY NO. 3

- Put a target on a wall (e.g., a snowman).
- Hit the snowman with a snowball for a point.

ACTIVITY NO. 4 GROUP

- Choose one or more people to be a "joke teller" or group leader, who will be the friendly target to this game.
- If the joker tells a not-so-funny joke (which is usually the case), then the players will have a great time throwing the soft snowballs at this person.

FILE FOLDER GAMES

File Folder Games are limitless, almost free, easy to make, easy to use, easy to store, transport and especially fun!

SAFETY PRECAUTION!

✓ Always supervise the Loved One when using scissors, magic markers and glue.

SUPPLIES:

- File Folders, any color
- Ziploc baggies
- Cards to match
- Magazine pictures
- Blunt scissors
- Magic markers
- Glue/glue sticks
- Stickers
- Copy paper

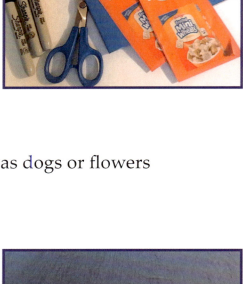

SUPPLIES: ACTIVITY NO. 1 MATCHING

- Playing cards with different pictures on the cards such as dogs or flowers
- A folder
- Glue
- Ziploc baggie

DIRECTIONS:

- Spread out and glue approximately 10 different card pictures on the inside of the folder.
- Make a deck of matching cards for the Loved One to match to the ones on the file folder.
- Have the Loved One take one card at time and match the card picture to the one in the folder.
- Store the loose cards in a Ziploc baggie.

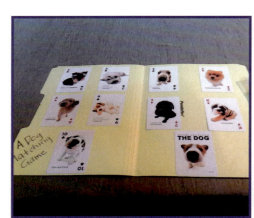

SUPPLIES: ACTIVITY NO. 2 FAMILY PICTURES MATCH

- Individual photos of family members
- File folder
- Glue
- Magic marker
- Ziploc baggie

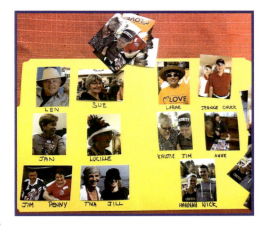

DIRECTIONS:

- Take the individual photos and make 2 prints of each.
- Glue one copy inside the file folder.
- Print the name of the family member under the photo.
- One at a time take the second copy of the photo and hand it to the Loved One to find the match.
- Talk about each photo as you are doing the activity with the Loved One.
- Store the loose photos in a Ziploc bag.

SUPPLIES: ACTIVITY NO. 3 SHAPES MATCH

- Copy paper
- Scissors
- Magic marker
- Card stock
- File folder
- Ziploc baggie
- Glue

DIRECTIONS:

- Take a piece of copy paper and divide it into
    12 sections by drawing the boxes on the paper.
- With the magic marker draw out different shapes.
- Glue the copy paper to the inside cover of the folder.
- Take a piece of card stock and cut into 12 boxes.
- With a magic marker draw the matching shape as seen on the copy paper.
- Store the card stock sections in a baggie.
- To use give one card stock shape to the Loved One and have them find the match.

SUPPLIES: ACTIVITY NO. 4 MAGAZINE PICTURES MATCH

- Purchase 2 magazines that are identical
- Scissors
- File folder
- Glue
- Ziploc baggie

DIRECTIONS:

- Locate a picture in the magazine.
- Find the same picture in the other magazine.
- Cut both pictures and set them aside.
- Repeat the process a few times.
- Take one set and glue them to the inside of the folder.
- Have the Loved One take the other set
  - one at a time- and find the match.
- Store the loose pictures in the baggie.

SUPPLIES: ACTIVITY NO. 5 COUNTING CARS

- File folder
- Copy paper
- Magic marker with several primary colors
- Glue
- Pencil

DIRECTIONS:

- Line out columns on a piece of copy paper.
- Draw and color 5 cars or so.
- Glue the copy paper of car drawings inside the folder.
- Looking out the window or sitting outside, count and record the cars.

SUPPLIES: ACTIVITY NO. 6 MAZES

- Magic marker
- Glue
- Folder
- Stickers
- Plain copy paper
- Pencil w/eraser

DIRECTIONS:

- Make two different mazes on copy paper. The way to do so is download "simple mazes" free from the internet.
- Glue a different maze on each inside cover of the file folder.
- Place a sticker at the beginning of the maze and a different one at the end.
- Guide the Loved One to take a pencil and start moving along the maze to the end.
- Erase the results to start over.

A TWIST ON "SIMON SAYS"

This is a twist on "Simon Says", making it a great game for exercising your brain and body. "Simon" says: clap your hands 3 times. "Simon" says: kick your right leg 2 times. "Simon" says: touch or point to something blue. Simon's commands can be adapted to each individual's skill level.

SAFETY PRECAUTION!

✓ If balance is an issue with the Loved One, sitting down playing the game is recommended and still a fun activity.

SUPPLIES:

- No supplies are needed
- Play where the Loved One can sit comfortably – living room or kitchen

DIRECTIONS:

- Caregiver will have to demonstrate this activity.
- Explain to the Loved One that "Simon" will give commands and they have to follow.
- Take turns being "Simon" if skill level permits.
- Give commands that exercise the Loved One physically: rub your stomach, pat your head, stomp your feet, etc. Tell how many times to do this action.
- Give commands that exercise the Loved One mentally: count to 15, repeat "I am an awesome person", touch something square, find the letter "R", roar like a lion, etc.
- If the Loved One's skill level permits, try leaving out "Simon says" occasionally… you've tricked them and then it is their turn to be "Simon".
- Use your imagination.

CARD GAMES
FUN FOR EVERYONE

Card games are for everyone! There are card games for all levels of play. Go Fish, Crazy Eight, Memory Game and War! Old Maid, UNO and Photo Cards! Games can be played using the original rules, or with very simple adaptations! There are so many benefits to playing cards: fine motor skills and eye-hand coordination improve, exercising your mind, and interaction with each other. Remember to have fun! Here are a few ideas.

SUPPLIES:

- 4+ decks of cards with a variety of designs on the back
- Optional: Poster board, cardboard or the inside blank side of cereal boxes
- Glue stick

DIRECTIONS: ACTIVITY NO. 1 MATCHING PICTURES

- Glue 6 or more cards, facing up, onto the poster board. The number you use depends on the skill level of the Loved One.
- Alternate using red/black cards to limit confusion.
- Gluing is optional. You can just lay them down.
- Using cards from the 2nd deck, the Loved One will match the cards that are laid down.
- The number of cards you give from the 2nd deck will be determined by the skill of the Loved One.

DIRECTIONS: ACTIVITY NO. 2 MATCHING NUMBERS

- Match and sort the backs of several different decks of cards.
- Match and sort using the numbers and symbols.
- Match and sort using red and black suits.
- UNO cards are great for matching.
- You can also print doubles of family pictures, glued to old cards, and play a family matching game.

DIRECTIONS: ACTIVITY NO. 3 UNO

- Play by the rules.
- Play with your own rules some ways include:
    - Sort by color.
    - Sort by number.
    - Sort by color and number.
    - The caregiver can reduce the size of the deck and play a simplified game with the original rules.

COME TO ME,
ALL YOU WHO
ARE WEARY AND
BURDENED AND I
WILL GIVE YOU REST

—MATTHEW 11:28

THINGS TO DO OUTSIDE

THERE IS BEAUTY AND JOY THAT SURROUNDS US.
STEP OUTSIDE AND SHARE A MOMENT, QUIETLY WITH THE LOVED ONE.

NATURE SIGHTSEEING

GOD'S PALLET

There are many ways to observe nature in all its beauty. You can simply sit out on a porch, in your yard, driveway or expand geographically out from there. Remember in a natural, quiet setting, concentrate on all the senses: sight, smell, hearing, taste & touch.

SUPPLIES:

- None necessary

DIRECTIONS:

- Start simply in your yard or driveway. Walk or sit and look around.
- Ask the Loved One if he/she sees or hears what you see or hear.
- Grab a hand full of grass, pick a flower or leaf.
- Share what you see, hear and smell with the Loved One.
- Make the Loved One aware of how the sun, wind, air temperature is sensed.
- Expand your sightseeing opportunities to consider beaches, lakes, city parks, zoos, mountains and a place to view beautiful sunsets.If you are limited with mobility much can be viewed while sitting in a car.

- There are other ways to see nature including:
  - Gardening or yard work.
  - Watching a couple of fish in a small fish bowl.
  - Feeding ducks and birds.
  - Going fruit picking for apples and berries.
  - Playing in snow.

THERE IS NO LIMIT TO THE WAY GOD CAN COMMUNICATE WITH YOU.

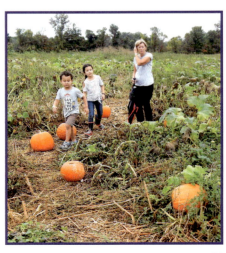

WALK ON THE BEACH

This is one of many types of nature outings that are healthy and enjoyable. Other destinations extend from your own backyard to paths through the woods, parks, etc.!

SAFETY PRECAUTION!

✓ Be very careful to evaluate the health, ability, energy, capacity and safety of the Loved One. Even just going out in the yard requires prior planning. Prior planning includes elements of transportation, food, water, the continuous needs of the Loved One and your own personal limitations and ability to take a Loved One outside. Taking along neighbors and friends is always to be considered.

SUPPLIES:

- Cellphone
- Proper clothing, possibly an extra coat
- Proper footwear
- Any assistive device such as: cane, walker or wheelchair
- People or a person to assist
- Sunglasses
- Water and possibly a snack
- Head cover such as: cap or hat
- A bag to hold found "treasures"
- A pre- prepared plan

DIRECTIONS:

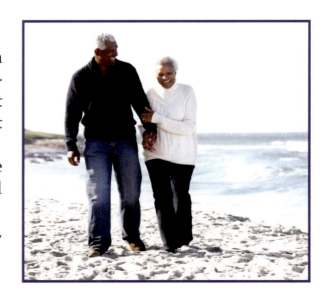

- As you prepare for your nature walk even though you have a plan, make a final assessment of your ability, the Loved One's current condition and the weather. If all is not perfect just put it off for another day.
- When at the beach you can often park in a place where you can sit and hear people talking and watch what they are doing.
  - Notice the action of the waves, the birds, clouds and other features of nature.

- If able you can venture out onto the beach. Searching for treasures is great. Sand, stones and shells are great treasures to be saved.
- Take time to sit in the sand and build a sand castle.
- Check with the Loved One often to see how they are doing. Do not go too far from the car. Keep it in sight. No need to walk far.
- This activity is for fresh air, seeing nature at its best and sharing. It is not for the purpose of "getting a workout" or exercise.
- Use your beach chairs, sit and enjoy.

OUR TRIPS... OUR STORIES
FUN FOR EVERYONE

A fun way to reminisce together! Telling stories about your trips, looking at pictures and making your stops on the map.

SAFETY PRECAUTION!

✓ Provide supervision when markers are being used.

SUPPLIES:

- Map of US and/or the World
- Notebook/pen
- Photos
- Markers

DIRECTIONS:

- Pick a place you have visited together.
- Find it on the map and mark it.
- Write down memories you have of this trip.
- Include pictures if you have any (Pictures might help remind the Loved One of the trip).
- This can be an ongoing together activity.

VEHICLES AND MORE. . .

Pull up a chair, sit on a bench and become vehicle, people and animal watchers!

SAFETY PRECAUTION!

✓ Watch out for traffic!

SUPPLIES:

- Clipboard
- Pencil/pen
- Paper
- Drawings of vehicles, pictures of cars, dogs, birds, etc.
- File Folders

DIRECTIONS:

- Download vehicle/animal/people pictures from the internet or draw your own.
- Make a simple chart to track numbers of vehicles/animals/walkers you see.
- You can also draw and color different cars and see how many of each color you see.
- Store and carry these games on a clipboard. Take them anywhere you go.

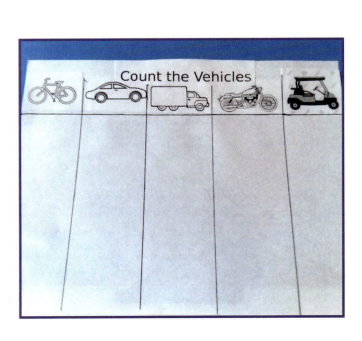

SEED PLANTING

Planting and taking care of the plants and watching them grow is a great activity. These plants are suggested for inside the house or porch so the Loved One can "keep an eye" on their growth.

SAFETY PRECAUTION!

✓ Seeds and dirt might look tempting to eat! Always be with the Loved One during this project!

SUPPLIES:

- Dirt (You can use potting soil, but plain dirt is good too)
- Bean seeds, marigold seeds, or grass seeds
- Clear plastic cup or glass jar
- Spoon
- Water

DIRECTIONS:

- Pick out the plants you would like to grow.
- Put dirt into cup or jar.
- With the handle of the spoon, poke some holes in dirt.
- Drop in seeds.
- Cover with dirt.
- Water.
- Watch your plant grow fast!

CELL PHONE WALK

SAFETY PRECAUTION!

✓ Do not wander too far.

SUPPLIES:

- A nice day outside
- Cell phone
- An assistive device as necessary, such as a walking stick, cane, wheelchair, etc.

DIRECTIONS:

- "Mosey" along slowly-very slowly, walk, amble or ride along. While doing so, take pictures with a cell phone and talk about what you see.
- As you move forward, focus on the things you sense around you.
- Look and point out flowers, clouds, birds, trees, houses, etc. Take time to study each one.
- Have the Loved One point to items of interest too.
- Take a cell phone picture of the things you talked about.
- Try to isolate each object from other distractions as much as possible.
- When you return, review and talk about the pictures you saw on your walk.

"OPTIMISM IS THE FAITH THAT LEADS TO ACHIEVEMENT"
— HELEN KELLER

FOOD FOR FOODIES

FUN TO DO ENJOYABLE TO EAT

ZIPLOC BAG OMELET(S)

FUN AND DELICIOUS

Most people agree, once you prepare an omelet in this way you will do it often. It is very easy and the omelet is delicious.

SAFETY PRECAUTION!

- ✓ This activity involves boiling water and hot contents in a Ziploc bag. Only the caregiver is to perform this part of the activity, regardless of the capabilities of the Loved One.
- ✓ All chopped vegetables should be prepared by the caregiver.

SUPPLIES:

- Quart size Ziploc bag
- Two eggs per person
- Variety of chosen ingredients such as:
  - diced onions
  - shredded cheese
  - chopped ham
  - bacon
  - sliced mushrooms
  - chopped sausage
- A two quart pot will accomodate 2 omelets.
- Tongs
- Pot holder or oven mitts
- Seasoning (salt, pepper or other)
- Scissors

DIRECTIONS:

- Fill pot half way with water.
- Crack open an egg and empty the contents into one Ziploc bag. Repeat so that there are two eggs in each Ziploc bag to serve each person.
- Seal the bag and have the Loved One mush the eggs together in the bag.
- The caregiver should open the bag and the Loved One select and add their ingredients.
- Close the bag again and have the Loved One mush together the contents. Make sure it's well sealed.
- Place the pot of water on the stove and bring it to a boil. (This is to be done by the caregiver only).
- Using the tongs place the bag(s) carefully into the boiling water.

- Boil for seven (7) minutes.
- Turn off the stove.
- With the tongs, remove the Ziploc bags from the pot and place on a plate. (Safely keep this step of the activity away from the Loved One).
- Hold the bag with the tongs or oven mitt, and with the scissors cut open the bag. (Caution: bag and contents are very hot)
- Hold the corners of the bottom of the bag using the oven mitt and slide the omelet onto a plate.
- Season as desired.
- Serve toast with butter, jelly or cinnamon sugar if desired.

MAKE AND DECORATE CUPCAKES

Cupcakes or muffins are easy to make and fun to decorate and as always the goal is to have an enjoyable activity together regardless of what the end process may look like.

SAFETY PRECAUTION!

✓ All parts of this activity around a hot oven must be performed by the caregiver with the Loved One at a safe distance.

SUPPLIES:

- Cake mix with listed ingredients on box
- Ready-made frosting
- Muffin pan with liners
- Large mixing bowl
- Mixer
- Spatula
- Spoons
- Oven Mitts
- Cooling rack
- Jellybeans
- M & M's
- Sprinkles
- Chocolate bits
- Mini marshmellows
- Candies
- Other decorations

DIRECTIONS:

- Following the directions on the cake mix box.
- Put liners in muffin pan.
- Fill each liner with 2/3 of the mix.
- Bake for 20 minutes at 350°.
- Remove from oven with oven mitts.
- Cool cupcakes completely on rack before decorating.
- Spread the frosting onto the top of the cupcakes with the spatula.
- Decorate cupcakes with choices listed or anything else your heart desires.
- Enjoy!

COFFEE CUP MICROWAVE SCRAMBLED EGGS

This activity is so simple to do, and the eggs are so fluffy and enjoyable you may never scramble eggs any other way in the future.

SAFETY PRECAUTION!

✓ Make sure the cup is microwave safe. When removing the cup (which must be microwave safe) from the microwave the cup and contents will be very hot. Let it cool or remove the eggs from the cup on a plate before eating.

SUPPLIES:

- Two (2) eggs per person and per cup
- Milk
- Spice as desired such as salt, pepper and cinnamon
- Oven mitts
- One (1) large microwave safe coffee cup
- Spoon

DIRECTIONS:

- Take two (2) eggs, break and empty the contents into the coffee cup.
- Add a touch of milk.
- Whip the milk and eggs until blended.
- Place into the microwave and heat on high for one (1) minute.
- Remove the cup from the microwave with oven mitts.
- Stir the contents of the cup until blended.
- Place the cup back into the microwave and heat on high for fifteen(15) seconds.
- Remove the cup with oven mitts and scoop the contents into a plate.
- Season as desired.

ENGLISH MUFFINS PIZZA

A SIMPLE AND YUMMY ACTIVITY

This is a great skill building activity. The Loved One will feel helpful and proud of their pizza.

SAFETY PRECAUTION!

✓ The caregiver should pre-cut all the toppings before doing the activity.

SUPPLIES:

- English muffins
- Pizza sauce
- Shredded mozzarella cheese
- Assortment of toppings: peppers, onion, mushrooms, ham, pepperoni, pineapple, etc.
- Oven cookie sheet

DIRECTIONS:

- Wash fresh toppings.
- Place the English Muffin halves onto a cookie sheet.
- Spoon pizza sauce onto the muffin halves.
- Add the toppings and mozzarella cheese.
- Bake for 10 minutes or until cheese is melted. (320°)
- Cool slightly, eat and enjoy!

IT'S NOT JUST PUDDING

It's a together project. It's a yummy delicious project.

SAFETY PRECAUTION!

✓ The caregiver should pre-cut the ingredients to be used.

SUPPLIES:

- Instant Pudding
- Milk
- Toppings such as:
    - strawberries
    - blueberries
    - bananas
    - granola
    - broken pretzels
    - whipped cream
- Wisk
- Spoons

DIRECTIONS:

- Mix pudding according to directions on the box.
- Talk about the different toppings and pick what you would like to use.
- Layer toppings and pudding or just put toppings on top.
- Chill for a short time.

"MOST OF US HAVE MORE COURAGE THAN WE EVER DREAMED WE POSSESSED"

— DALE CARNEGIE

MUSIC TO MY EARS

MUSIC CAN:
REDUCE ANXIETY AND DEPRESSION REDUCE AGITATION
RELIEVE STRESS STIMULATE ACTIVITY RECALL MEMORIES

MUSIC! MUSIC! MUSIC!

Music has many benefits for Loved Ones with Alzheimer's. Music can assist Loved Ones with emotional and behavioral challenges. Dr. Jonathan Graff- Radford of the Mayo Clinic has published numerous studies which conclude that "brain areas, linked to musical memory are relatively less affected by the disease".

MUSIC TIPS:

- When planning a variety of music observe the Loved One's reaction to determine what music or types of music illicit a positive response. Play music the Loved One likes, and also knows the words.
- Be mindful that the volume of played music is extremely important. Played too softly the Loved One may not hear it; played too loudly may result in increased agitation, confusion and stress.
- When you determine what music and volume is enjoyed by the Loved One play it often.
- Music may assist the Loved One during challenging times, such as bathing, by being a calming influence.
- Be mindful that competing noise is most always anxiety provoking. Television in one area, competing with people talking, competing with traffic noise, competing with music in any combination at any time will increase anxiety, stress and discomfort for most of us, but to a greater extent for Loved Ones with the challenges of illness.
- Do not play music that has commercials. Commercials interrupt the Loved One's focus, mood and can be confusing.

SING ALONG
AN UPLIFTING ACTIVITY

The Loved One may well retain the ability to sing along and enjoy this activity longer than you can imagine.

SUPPLIES:

- The voices of the Loved One and caregiver
- A little knowledge of some "old" simple, familiar songs Example: God Bless America, America The Beautiful
- DVD'S such as:
  - Sing along with Suzie Q   www.beemusicstudios.com
  - Music for the mind and heart by Katherine Griffin
      www.musicforthemindandheart.com
  - Memory Lane Therapy memorylanetherapy.com
  - Sing Along For Seniors melodicmemories.com
- Google or YouTube Songs Examples:
  - Rio's Seniors Sing-along-upbeat
  - Sing Along with Seniors w/printed words
  - Senior Sing Alongs - Dawn Rence
  - Sing Along Elderly Songs
  - What a Friend We Have in Jesus w/lyrics.
  - If you're happy and you know it…
  - 101 Songs (w/lyrics) You Know By Heart
  - John Mc Sweeney

DIRECTIONS:

- Sing loud, sing often, enjoy.

MUSIC ENCOURAGING MOVEMENT

SAFETY PRECAUTION!

✓ Be careful not to overstimulate or create movement beyond the capability of the Loved One. Make it enjoyable and safe. Be specifically mindful of the potential for the Loved One to lose balance, fall or injure themself.

SUPPLIES:

• Music

DIRECTIONS:

• Caregiver can encourage and direct the following movements:
• Clapping hands
• Tapping feet
• Drumming on a flat surface with fingers and hands
• Chair dancing- while sitting, move arms, legs, and body to the beat of the music. (Be careful that the Loved One is safely seated so as not to fall on the floor).
• Dancing (Be mindful of the Loved One's strength and balance, of tripping and falling hazards and the potential of a Loved One falling).
• Drumming with a safe object on the bottom of an overturned rubber bucket or container.

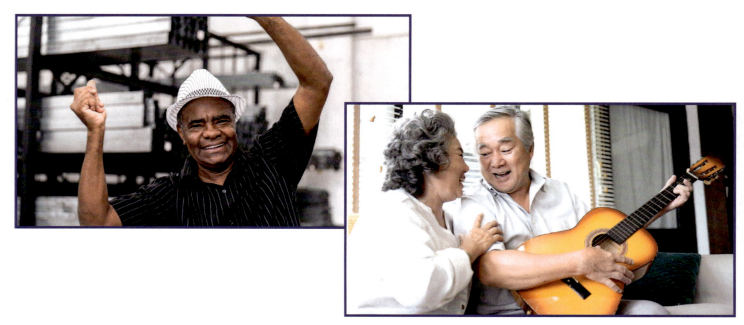

MUSICAL INSTRUMENTS: SHAKERS

This is a fun and free activity to do with the Loved One that will enable him/her to "shake" along with any kind of music.

SAFETY PRECAUTION!

✓ Always be with the Loved One when filling the empty containers. He/she may try putting some of the items into their mouth. After filling the containers, seal well with a glue gun or very sticky tape.

SUPPLIES:

- Empty vitamin/supplement containers (hand held size)
- Empty plastic spice containers
- Colored paper, stickers, markers
- Glue stick, glue gun, tape, scissors
- Dry rice, beans, popcorn kernels, old beads… things that make noise

DIRECTIONS:

- Remove all items from containers.
- Wash and dry containers.
- Decorate as desired, with colored paper, markers, stickers.
- Fill each one with noisy items, such as dried rice, dried beans, even old beads.
- Secure lid using a hot glue gun or very sticky tape such as duct tape or mailing tape.
- SHAKE, SHAKE, SHAKE to different kinds of music and with different sounding containers!!

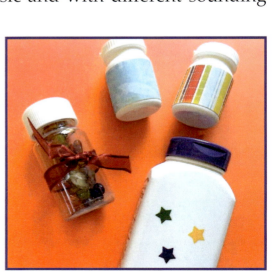

THE LORD CALLED UPON NUMEROUS PEOPLE TO ASSIST IN THE CREATION OF THIS BOOK. THEY INCLUDE:

Susan and Linwood Galeucia
TEACHER/HOSPITAL ADMINISTRATOR

Jan Pandy
TEACHER/SOCIAL WORKER

Lucille Jesaitis
NURSE

Vicki and Charlie Yates
TEACHER/FACILITIES ADMINISTRATOR

Kristie and Jim Faison
ACTIVITIES DIRECTOR/EQUIPMENT REPAIR

Jean & Chuck Hudson
FORMER BUSINESS OWNERS

Jill Galeucia & Tina Underwood
JEWELRY BENCH JEWELER/
EDUCATION ADMINISTRATOR

John & Betty Suprenant
RESTAURANT OWNER/TEACHER

LaRae Donnellan
COMMUNICATION SPECIALIST

Louise & Carl Shuey
EXECUTIVE DIRECTOR ALZHEIMER'S
ASSOCIATION/AIRPLANE MECHANIC

Bill Osborn
ELECTRICAL ENGINEER

Hannah & Nick
STUDENTS

Mike & Angie Galeucia
MARKETING SPECIALIST/
BUSINESS OWNER

Peter Toppen
PAPER PRODUCT SALES

Jim & Penny Hoppe
WORKMAN COMP.
MANAGER/COSMETOLOGIST